Coffee
Shop
Musings

Coffee Shop Musings

*A Collection of Little Rhythmic
Thoughts Unbound by Convenience*

Simon I. Perlsweig

ISBN: 978-1-09835-229-5 Paperback
ISBN: 978-1-09835-230-1 eBook

This book is dedicated to all those friends who have followed and supported my writing endeavors both academically and creatively.

Table of Contents

Preface

One of the great things about being an author is that there is the freedom to dabble in as many or as few genres and styles as one desires. Back when my first book, *Front Porches to Front Lines*, was nearing completion, I regularly found myself working on it steadily for several hours each day before a point came when the ideas and words simply stopped flowing. When this happened, I found myself sitting at my desk, just staring off into space and unable to type another word. Put more simply, I was having these bouts of writer's block and the creative juices simply ceased to function. Knowing that the deadlines to get the manuscript for my first book submitted so that it could be ready for its November 11, 2018 release date were fast approaching, I began to ponder any and all possible solutions to this rather perplexing problem. It was at this time that I wondered if spending some time working with another genre of writing might be the trick. It was then, that I began to writing poetry on a regular basis, usually these short, three-line poetic thoughts, many of which occupy the pages of this book. After trying this trick out for about a week and seeing how successful it was, I started writing these three-line poems on a regular basis every morning before diving into my history writing for the remainder of each day. What follows are about 300 of these little poems, many of which I shared with friends and family in order to get their thoughts and feedback. The reason for the title, *Coffee Shop Musings*, is because most of them were written while sitting in local coffee shops instead of at my desk at my home. I hope you enjoy and draw pleasure and inspiration from these little nuggets of poetry.

Simon Perlsweig
November 2020

Coffee
Shop
Musings

Number One
The One Which Started It All

Friend

While people are many,
like small grains of sand,
Friends are much fewer,
like the fingers on one's hands,
And a true friend is rare –
one makes a band.

Personal & People

Good Night! (17/18)
Today's a success, it's time to renew,
For body and soul, one's character too,
With that let me say, "Good Night!" to you.

Today's a success, it's time to renew,
For a new day, new challenges too,
On that note, I'll say, "Good Night!" to you.

The Three Stooges (38/39/40)
Most of the wits with a tongue like a blade,
On top of most things, except when afraid,
Even his slapstick has a price to be paid.

Long, frizzy hair, in dire need of a comb,
With a similar beard, he'd look like a gnome,
Risks are his game, on jobs in the home.

Clumsy he is and known for being rotund,
Unusual things get him sparked on the run,
Real good in a fight, his gut is his gun.

Frozen Fingers (54)
Forgot to wear gloves, I know that was dumb,
From white, pink to red, my fingers turned numb,
A hot drink is the cure, perhaps coffee or rum.

The Girl at 58 (55)
Five foot four, with a demeanor so fair,
A cheery smile, with long, curly, black hair,
A gem of a friend, with so much to share.

Zero Degrees (34)
Stepping out for a walk, into the freeze,
Body shivers all over, from teeth to knees,
No wonder I'm cold, it's zero degrees.

Little Icicles (35)
Despite warm socks, it's cold I still know,
They are so numb, that's just how it goes,
Such is the tale of ten icicle toes.

My Desk is a Mess (59)
Piled with papers, empty space is none,
Pens everywhere, please walk, don't run,
Clearing up this chaos, needs three days, not one.

Bottles Scattered (74)
In a yard down the street, a large tree was cut down,
When removed, beer bottles were found,
Kids likely, after a night on the town.

Left Hand Table (80)

At the table to my left, there is much talk,
Mostly complaints, by people who squawk,
My ears get a rest, when half the crowd walks.

Zoo (91)

In each pen or tank, there's a creature not tame,
The kids who are there, are known to act the same,
A head scratcher it is, when the monkey's more-
tame.

Snow Shoveling (106)

Out the window I look, there's white on the ground,
By the time the job's done, I've got aches all around,
Hot water for tea is a welcoming sound.

Patience (107)

Waiting can be tough, it can feel like a crime,
Some wish that all things, would take place on a
dime,
Though it's said the best things, will come in good
time.

The Old Pair of Boots (108)

Sturdy and worn, always there when in need,
Of durable leather, from cowhide some breed,
We've been through a lot, good and bad deeds.

The Bank Teller (117)
Behind a high desk, with a greet and grin,
Most things she solves, or she chuckles with
chagrin,
Maintaining her cool, when there's tension within.

Detective (123)
Takes on the tough cases, those of sin and shame,
Sometimes there's a case, lacking in names,
Those who survive, hidden is their fame.

Missing Word (130)
Texting is great, though it has a pitfall,
A word goes missing, through the cracks it falls,
"You're too hard on yourself", says a friend not
appalled.

Shower (135)
What goes on within shouldn't always be shared,
Some like to sing, others think well in there,
A personal rain, to cleanse body and hair.

Two Girls (137)
At a side table, two girls chatter away,
For us who are grown, we smile and say,
Oh, what a sight, with innocence at play.

Barista (139)
Walk thru the door, get greeted by name,
Order's all in, some mind reading game,
The warmth is two-fold, so glad I came.

Pocket Watch (141)
At the end of a chain, often silver or gold,
Your grandfather's it was, so it's got to be old,
A timeless treasure, you've been entrusted to hold.

Well-Traveled Hat (144)
Rough 'round the edges, though still in one piece,
It's been through a lot - many sprays, gels and
grease,
All over it's been, a source of joyous release.

Chasing My Hat (148)
A strong gust came up, took it right off my head,
I ran through many yards, quite a journey it led,
Coming to rest, on the peak of my shed.

Snowman (154)
Of packed ice and snow, decorated all ways,
In all sizes and shapes, cold weather kids' play,
There to enjoy, until they're melted away.

Slept Thru My Alarm (160)

It went off long ago, but my bed was so warm,
Now I'm rushing, to get to work at the norm,
Multitasking is hard when time is like a bee swarm.

Sore Muscles (162)

In from the cold and I'm sore head to toe,
Such is the case from shoveling snow,
Let me fall in the chair with a cup of cocoa.

Committee (177)

Bodies of people, with an agenda to fill,
Meetings are fun, what's done is little,
Debates will ensue, a bystander's thrill.

Rick (184)

He owned a cafe, where much more went on,
Gambling and sales amidst romantic bonds,
The political game, he had never been fond.

Oh I'm Tired (206)

It's been a long day, I'd like to collapse in place,
Since six this morning, things have felt like a race,
Long weekend is needed to come down from this
pace.

A New Friend (231/232)
Came to a conference and at times felt alone,
Took lots of notes, til my hands groaned,
And made a new friend, which set a new tone.

We came to network, totally unaware,
With a Georgian belle, a local guy got paired,
Fast friends we were, lunch and coffee we shared.

Slow Steady Stroll (208)
On a Sunday in March, a warm spring day,
Sixty degrees and the world is at play,
As we cherish this time, the wind leads the way.

Conference Life (210)
Lectures and sessions, networking and tours,
By the end of each day, all feet are quite sore,
New friends and culture, open countless new doors.

Crazy Relatives (211)
We've all got a couple, you know who they are,
View all your moves as strange and bizarre,
You're thankful they live many miles afar.

Train Atrium (212)
In a room so wide, so high and so long,
A rainbow of people keeps moving along,
There's plenty of room as the feet tap up a song.

The Last Man in the Bar (214)
Early in the morning, about a quarter to three,
The room's gone quiet and it's too dark to see,
And with the bartender is the whiskey and me.

Within the Fog (221)
With a light and a horn, to guide ships away,
The lighthouse stands tall, its job is not play,
Its keeper is old, like the fog he has grayed.

Types of Waiting (241)
Exciting is one, annoying is two,
Publisher is the second, tore my hair out too,
And coffee's the first, with a friend such as you.

Pedestrian (243)
In the street corners, just waiting to cross,
Mostly innocent, but by some they are glossed,
Becoming live targets, leaves them at a loss.

A Guiding Light (244)
On a long lonely road, in the dark of night,
With dinner to walk off, we each glow so bright,
Oh, to be a friend, and a guide tonight.

A Stroll on the Beach (245)
Sand between toes, of crabs and shells beware,
Waves hit the shore, a gentle breeze through hair,
A time well spent, when with friends it's shared.

Running in Heels (246)
Perhaps as a guy, made this idea seem bizarre,
Especially indoors, on ground cool and hard,
A head-scratcher of sorts, accepted as they are.

Jewelry (250)
Of silver and gold, glistening in the sun,
Marking special times, those of joy and fun,
Gentle reminders of good feelings won.

Throne (276)
A chair colored gold, for some heads of state,
To receive his subjects, he sits and awaits,
A sign of great power, to be respected all dates.

Just a Phone Away (280)
By call or by text, the message gets through,
Answered in good faith, a reply pure and true,
When friendship is strong, the phone line is too.

Census Taker (286)
A thankless job, which needs to be done,
Meet all kinds of chaps, from the mean to the fun,
Be ready to chat or leave on the run.

Where's the Professor? (292)
Twenty minutes in and he's nowhere in sight,
Pen twirling is common, to the left and the right,
Then the word comes, "Class is canceled tonight".

A Bear Crossed My Path (293)
On an old town road, so quiet and fair,
The hour was early, there was much sun to share,
Thought I was alone, til I twice saw a bear.

A Friend, True and Rare (295)
People are many, like small grains of sand,
A few are called friends, they're a circular clan,
But a true friend is rare, one makes a band.

Second Chance (298)
Even though you were wronged, please take a soft
stance,
Though I know you're upset, it takes two to dance,
All I'm asking you for, is friendship's second
chance.

Small Talk (301)
While some talk is deep, other topics are light,
Despite certain claims, we've thus far done all right,
Our conversing's a joy, even late at night.

Break-up Phoenix (302)
Three months ago, I didn't know what to do,
After eighty weeks, I had to begin anew,
And oh how I feel blessed for having met you.

Grumpy Grandpa (242)
Sitting in a corner, with a perpetual scowl,
If he says anything, at least one word is foul,
The young he scares off - no future where he
prowls.

Philosophical

Crunch Time (3)
Deadlines are coming, they always do.
Although it's crunch time, I know you'll pull
through.
Just believe in yourself, your friends already do.

No Look or Hear (43)
There's a wily group known as senseless foes,
They lack eyes and ears, and often a nose,
Threats to all those who love their fingers and toes.

Just Go Away (49)
Rattling on, talking nonstop all day,
On bits of nothing, got no interest today,
Do these ears a favor and just go away.

Fountain (50)
A quencher of thirsts, where great wealth may be
found,
Where wishes on coins, are tossed all around,
A spring for our wants, ones like new knowledge
are sound.

Atmosphere (53)
There's a phrase many know, "There's something in
the air",
If we're all at peace, no tempers will flare,
Cheery moods will be found and pleasantness
shared.

Holding the Door (92)
Holding the door is a nice thing to do,
Until recently, the ways it got done were two,
Until I saw one held open, by an inflated balloon.

Tradition or Change (97)
Some people insist on sticking to the old ways,
The old rules are the best, for the game so they say,
But it's those who adapt who will win and still play.

Til Then (133)
A chance will come, it certainly will,
For a quiet drink, sharing tales to thrill,
Patience is key for friendship to be tilled.

Kindness (171)
Any small act, brings new light to the day,
Radiance is the smile, much warmth it displays,
Forever growing, a redemptive pathway.

Fly on the Wall (191)
Up in the corner, on the crown molding,
Sits a winged vault, with many stories and things,
A trove of secrets, always listening.

Peace (238)
A noble goal, which can be said many ways,
Even when it is reached, it seems so far away,
Given all its impacts, it's no matter of play.

The Seventh Sense (247)
We all know the five: see, touch, taste, hear, smell,
Then there's the sixth, intuition so tells,
There's a seventh one too - what to wear to look
swell.

Fashion Sense (248)
Elusive to most guys, most gals know it well,
Points to the guy, who heeds the words a girl tells,
Since two looks better, then one bad plus one swell.

Monday, Maybe 13, 2019 (249)
As odd as this is, I promise it's true,
A message on my phone, left me asking, "Who
knew?",
Of a thirteenth month, for a second or two.

Friendship Triangle (273)
Your presence is felt, no matter where you are.
Support is heartfelt, from near or afar.
Friendship is divine, on a very high bar.

Sprang Back to Life (289)
It sat on the mantel, had been silent so long,
Was right twice a day, without playing its song,
When out of the blue, came tick-tock and ding-
dong.

Jewish & Religious

Christmas Time (2)

It's Christmas time, the snow and cold are here.
For many a Jew, it's another day in the year.
One for Chinese and movies, and mitzvot to spread
cheer.

Shabbat Candles (5)

Like two little beacons, glistening and bright,
Welcoming the Shabbat queen each Friday night,
Whose presence is honored with joyous songs of
delight.

Torah (6)

These five books of Moses, give guidance each day,
The tav in tanach is full of wisdom to stay,
With the oral tradition, it shows us the way.

Challah (7)

Braided loaves of eggs, flour and yeast,
The kickoff staple of each holiday feast,
The key to one's lips, to say the least.

Shabbat Walk (9)

Friday or Saturday, morn, noon and night,
To be at one with your thoughts, in the Lord's sight,
A time to reflect amongst creation's delights.

The Ark (15)
For forty days, one held Noah and pairs,
One floated Moses, til Pharaoh's daughter took
care,
The third holds the Torah, in shuls here to there.

Sunrise (21)
At dawn it's light welcomes the day,
A cheerful sight on an eastward foray,
"Let there be light!", so did the Lord say.

Kosher (33)
Chews cud with split hooves, has scales and fins,
Some fit only half, their consumption is sin,
Every dish can be made, so that it fits in.

Jerusalem (47)
Heart of a nation, a city of gold,
Where the temple once stood, all its glory foretold,
Stands a sign, of perseverance so bold.

Mezuzah (48)
Upon the doorpost, with the tiniest words,
On the power of faith, being seen, it is heard,
A sign he protects, when we leave and enter.

Prayer (52)

A spiritual bond, communal or alone,
Wants and needs are expressed, no need of a phone,
With faith and belief, may they all become known.

The 3 T's (Tefillin, Tallit, Tzitzit - 30/31/32)

Little black boxes with verses inside,
Signs on our hands and over our eyes,
That the Lord is all over and on every side.

A colorful shawl - black, blue and white,
In what Isaac was wrapped, at Rivkah's first sight,
Worn as we pray - most days and a night.

Pretty, little fringes of white and blue,
A sign that the Lord watches all that we do,
And of all the mitzvot, held dear by Jews.

Abraham & Sarah (41/42)

Abraham, our father, was the very first Jew,
In one g-d he believed, even as a kid too,
His tests numbered ten, each time he came through.

Sarah, his wife, had beauty beyond years,
A prophetess too, one of seven revered,
Each of her days was joyous with cheer.

Purim (62)
Silliness and noise, costumes and treats,
No need to feel shame, if on tipsy feet,
Blessed or cursed, confusion's so sweet.

Commentary (63)
Growing each day for thousands of years,
Muddying waters or a new path it clears,
Nice for a listen or hitting closed ears.

Kiddush Glass (67)
A blessing of praise, said over good wine,
Considered to be, a drink of the divine,
A kick start to the meal, the first thing that's dined.

Sinai (69)
A hill among peaks, where the law was received,
It's calling card is humble, our first act we deceived,
Our thanks goes to Moses, for in us he believed.

Laundry List (70)
So much to do, too much for one day,
Some of said work, has the feeling of play,
Thankfully there's Shabbat, for that list goes away.

Psalms (71)

Songs of great praise for noteworthy highlights,
Of people and places, of events and great sights,
An integral aspect, of prayer day and night.

Star of David (73)

A six-pointed shape, triangles times two,
An ancient symbol, the State of Israel renewed,
A rallying emblem, for thousands of Jews.

Lulav and Etrog (75)

Four species they are, from the holy land,
Heart, eyes, mouth and spine - for which they stand,
Shaken all ways - when clutched in our hands.

Afikomen (76)

A large piece of matzah, the kids seek all around,
Could be anywhere, up high or low down,
The more kids there are, the faster it's found.

Dreidel (79)

A four-sided top, one letter per side,
A clever disguise, there was learning to hide,
Jewish gambling, amidst yuletide.

Gragger (81)
Little noise makers to blot out a name,
Sometimes there's a kid who needs to be tamed,
Who's having much fun and covers all names.

Hallel (83)
A selection of Psalms, words of great praise,
Reserved to be sung, on the happiest days,
A time to reflect while our spirits get raised.

Latkes (84)
Potatoes and oil are the core of this dish,
Fried in a hot pan, there's more if you wish,
A Hannukah staple, a culinary niche.

Shavua Tov (85)
Rested all day, a new week has come,
The food tasted real good, even the crumbs,
And "Shavua Tov" is the tune we all hum.

Matzah (86)
Flour and water, that's the simplest it gets,
Unleavened and hard, baked hot so it sets,
Is yeast legal tender to pay off a debt?

Maror (87)
Bitter and hot, a fire lit in your throat,
Recalling hard labor, every year we take note,
Keep water on hand, perhaps a large tote.

Pesach (93)
Eight days without bread, which can get old quick,
Adapting good dishes can be quite a trick,
Success is the truth when the plates are well licked.

Succah (100)
A temporary house, lived in for eight days,
An all-natural place, to eat, sleep and play,
Except when the rain keeps us away.

10 Commandments (101)
Solid statutes to live by every day,
Received at Sinai, on two tablets they say,
We all heard the first two, the last eight got relayed.

Mitzvot (102)
Six hundred thirteen is their total so grand,
To our everyday lives, applied they all can,
They're all in the Torah, to adhere is the plan.

Tu B'Av (103)
The Jewish version of Valentine's Day,
Joy and miracles are hallmarks today,
The grape harvest it marks and girls dancing so gay.

Tu B'Shevat (104)
A celebration of fruits, a time to plant trees,
Some have a seder, with good wine and species,
Nature's new year, one of four Jewishly.

Shul (131)
To connect with the Lord, each in their own way,
In the midst of the law, makes for meaningful stays,
Alone and with others are two ways to pray.

Lag Baomer (152)
Day thirty-three, in a stretch known for bans,
A cheerful respite, amidst this seven-week span,
Celebrations are many, much eloping gets planned.

Two Names (161)
There are many things which set apart the Jews,
Kosher, Shabbat and our second names too,
The Hebrew one's special, it's the essence of you.

Bityah (118)

The daughter of Pharaoh, she was a rebel,
Defying her father, when she pulled from the
swells,
A boy in the Nile, tucked in a woven vessel.

Proverbs (119)

A collection of wisdom, sayings, anecdotes,
Words to live by, passages of note,
None more than "Eishet Chayil", each week many
quote.

Havdalah (125)

It's Saturday night, Shabbat's nearing its end,
A torch of a candle waves farewell to a friend,
Til next Friday night, when she'll be welcomed
again.

Two Leading Pillars (127)

There was fire by night and smoke by day,
On a forty-year trek, the divine led the way,
With Moses his servant, transmitting the teachings
relayed.

In an Image (170)
On creation's sixth day, the human was brewed,
In his image as one and then split into two,
To one day reunite, seeing all that we do.

Adar (173)
Happiness and joy, increasing thirty days,
Costumes and confusion, a jolly holiday,
An inspiring tale, much heroics at play.

Welcome to the Tribe (174)
The journey was long, but you made it through,
Your story's unique, worth telling too,
With many chapters and layers, like all of us Jews.

Hamantaschen (178)
Three cornered cookies, sweet hats so small,
Creative fillings, in the dough in tight balls,
Dozens are made, to be shared with all.

Shavuot (186)
An auspicious moment marked by these days,
Two of the ten we all heard the Lord say,
All Jews were there, not just those of today.

Shalach Manot (195)

Little baskets of gifts, a collection of treats,
Cookies and candy and other things sweet,
Spreading great joy, to the friends that you meet.

Friendship Triangle (274)

Your presence is felt, no matter where you are,
Your support is heartfelt, from near or afar,
A friend who's divine, that's how special you are.

Dvar (193)

To learn and to teach - expanding what we all know,
Once you've done one, the easier they'll go,
With a message so strong, what will be the next
show.

Chametz Search (219)

With feather and flame, outside and in,
Check all the cracks and the corners within,
The leaven goes out, when the matzah comes in.

The Jew in Judaism (187)

Just thousands of pages, with volumes to go,
Each of us is a piece in an image that grows,
We each have some space to make our story be
known.

Rabbi, Priest & Imam (201/202/203)

Interpreter of the law, a leader of Jews,
Each question's a chance to learn something new,
Like his followers, he has his flaws too.

As the head of a church, a hard life lives he,
To help people soul search, forgiveness is key,
Abstentions are many, such as celibacy.

A leader of a faith, the youngest of the big three,
A faith with two sects, tensions are many,
Turbans are worn, a trademark of thee.

Dome (217)

A circular arch on a bubble of air,
A religious rooftop, where prayer gets shared,
It pleases the eye, should one happen to stare.

Blessed or Cursed (192)

The one time of year, getting drunk is allowed,
Where confusion ensues, and things can get loud,
And one name's blotted out, amidst a story with
shrouds.

Passover Cleaning (220)

Break out the vacuum, the brush, rag and broom,
Passover's coming - got to clean every room,
Then brighten each space with some pretty spring
blooms.

Jews on Christmas (223)

Chinese food, the movies, are just two of the ways,
The places they're found with their neighbors so
gay,
How Jews spend their time on each Christmas day.

Counting the Omer (224)

The seders are done, let the weeks begin,
Forty-nine are the days, ripe with abstentions,
On the fiftieth day, Shavuot rolls in.

Kosher Kitchen (235)

Filled with good food, its smells fill every room,
A lab of some sorts, where creativity blooms,
Each one is a book, where knowledge will loom.

Friendship (239)

A gift from the Lord, to get one through the day,
Mystical bonds, to be cherished always,
Strong but glassy, full of fun, joy and play.

The Lion's Den (240)
The author is Daniel, armed with words and a pen,
The publisher is a prick, with his own lions' den,
Sanity is salvaged with each text from a friend.

Siddur (256)
A book of prayers, texts and readings,
An inspiring source, with many songs to sing,
For the highs and lows, and all else the year brings.

Shabbat (262)
One day out of seven, we stop all that we do,
To learn, pray and eat, perhaps sleep a bit too,
A celebration of rest, Shabbat is to the Jews.

Yad (268)
Long and silver, with a chain on one end,
On the other a hand, from yours it extends,
For reading the law, it's always a friend.

Holiday Light (258)
For some it's twelve days, for others eight nights,
Both bring much cheer and to faces, delight,
Winter joy amidst snow and many sources of light.

Carb-Crazed Cat (285)

Be it muffins or bread, or perhaps crackers or cake,
Could be in a bag, or just having been baked,
Get out of the challah, for goodness sake!

Walk to Shul (287)

On a Saturday morn, about ten twenty-eight,
I scurry to shul, feeling blessed and quite great,
Here's to hoping the rabbi, will not realize I'm late.

Shabbat Glow (291)

Pleasing the eye, a shine of heavenly gold,
Inviting aromas, to warm body and soul,
Songs of great joy, bring the queen home from shul.

Rosh Hashanah (296)

A Jewish new year, one of four it is true,
On the old calendar, the year is half through,
The first two of ten days, to atone and renew.

Yom Kippur (297)

A day to atone, for our past wrong-dos,
A day to forgive, those sins done unto,
A fast and prayer, a long day in shul too.

Dinah (299)
A girl among boys, ratio twelve to one,
Kidnapped as a lass, so two brothers had fun,
Though rescued she was, their actions were shunned.

Friendship (300)
A gift from the Lord, or so says a verse,
Strength is its blessing, fragility it's curse,
Can be built fast or slow, it's parties diverse.

Christmas Music (303)
Songs of the season - Spreading joy, drying blues,
Heard everywhere, as good spirits ring true,
One thing that is strange, some well-known are by Jews.

Simchat Torah (257)
Dance with the five books, as it ends and begins,
The first and last letters, reveal the heart that's within,
New year means new learning, from the oral and written.

Walk from Shul (288)
Kiddush is over, we've all had a small munch,
The crowd leaves the shul, in many a bunch,
Where each hosting home, serves a warm, tasty lunch.

Hannukah Cheer (304)
Eight days long, a celebration of light,
Of latkes and gelt, there's much oil in sight,
And doughnuts all types, dreidels spinning all night.

The Flow of Torah (37)
A scroll's waterfall, from our tongues and our cheeks,
To where ideas get grown, when taught and then tweaked,
The "X" on the map, is the new knowledge we seek.

Dove (68)
A white feathered peace, an emissary of man,
Under a band of colors, seeking out dry land,
So dozens of pairs, could start rebuilding their clans.

Burning Bush (77)

Not consumed by the flame, a voice came from within,
At the base of a mount, uniquely destined,
Enlisting a shepherd, for a special mission.

Quest & Discovery

Research (4)
The quest for knowledge is so noble and true.
From uncovering the past to discovering the new.
It's wealth so deep, the sky's no limit too.

Writing (8)
The expression of words with pen and paper,
The insurance one needs to remember,
Preserving one's thoughts, a noble endeavor.

History (36)
Tales from the past with lessons to be learned,
Guidance for each day, with each step and turn,
Laying the future's groundwork is its main concern.

Index (72)
A collection of words, places and names,
At the end of most books, all looking the same,
In columns with pages, that's how they're framed.

Idea (82)
From where they come, is anyone's guess,
Nowhere is the place, known to spawn the best,
Sometimes they pop up, with no way to attest.

School (88)
A place of learning, knowledge passed on,
A place to make friends, help each other along,
For sharing this journey, is something to be fond.

Sphinx (179)
Lion and man combined in one pose,
Overlooking Egypt to guard the pharaohs,
With just one question - "Where is my nose?"

Office (96)
At a desk with a book or in a lab with some cells,
Each room is ground zero with a story to tell,
With each new tidbit, human karma does swell.

Ruins (136)
Signs of the past, not looking their best,
Worn down by time, hosting hundreds of guests,
Full of stories, we hold the key to this chest.

Numbers (215)
Some are rational, such as 1, 2 and 3,
Irrational are others, such as pi and e,
There's one that's unknown, it's imaginary.

Writer's Desk (216)
Cluttered and messy with papers stacked high,
Organized chaos, to one set of eyes,
Where ideas are spawned, new words of the wise.

Painting (226)
The same exact scene can be portrayed many ways,
Setting and style are two factors at play,
Each one is right, worth being displayed.

The Copyright Thorn (230)
Published a book, the first one I wrote,
Despite annotations and lots of good notes,
Issues were raised, with the pictures and quotes.

Secrets (261)
Tiny bits of knowledge, into the vault they go,
Much like poker, feelings shouldn't show,
For trust here is implied, no one else is to know.

Success Tunnel (260)
The journey is long, but have no fear,
The reward is the light, grows increasingly near,
Celebrate this moment, and all that noise which you
hear.

Inspiration (60/61)
Under a rock or out of thin air,
Behind all that is done, can also be shared,
A great start to the day, found anywhere.

The motivation for much that is done,
The driving force when work becomes fun,
And if work feels like play, each day is won.

Research Fumes (281)
Though tired I am, I keep pressing on,
Despite hunger and thirst, and daylight long gone,
There are goals to be met, as the process moves on.

College (94)
Two to four years, and for some many more,
Two schools of learning com - much fun or a chore,
Those met on this trip, are friends to the core.

Letters (146)
The stories they hide are countless insights and
gems,
These eyes to the past are the most honest of them,
A primary source from which others do stem.

High School (205)
Four years of adventure, growth and fun,
A whole bunch of friends, there's a lot which gets
done,
A taste of adulthood, that leaves some people
stunned.

Words (90)
They come in handy, each and every day,
A key in this world, a common-sense play,
Writ, spoke or thought - they're expressed many
ways.

The Writer's Curses (270)
Each word is hard thought, though judgment can
lack,
When a word is hurtful, it strikes in two acts,
Impact breeds worry, and that's simply a fact.

<u>Nature</u>

Rainbow (12)

From light and water, colors come through,
Red, yellow, orange, green, purple and blue,
A sign to Noah that world peace may ensue.

Snow (13)

Like a sugar coating, it whitens the ground,
School gets closed, kids cheer all around,
See the great art: men, balls and mounds.

Sunset (22)

In a sea of color; yellow, orange and red,
A wonderful view for a long westward tred,
All's well for the sailor, if the sky glows red.

The Sun (24)

At dawn it rises in a colorful sea,
Amidst blue skies, its rays warm up thee,
At dusk it sets, a sight of heavenly glee.

Cats and Dogs (45)

Four legs and tail, with loads to say,
Loyalty's constant, even on your worst day,
A friend in the wings, with greetings always.

Blue Skies (51)

Blue skies overhead, clear smiles to see,
Clouds with a pink glow, so wispy and free,
Bright and serene, sparking feelings of glee.

Seasons (WSSF - 26/27/28/29)

The weather is cold, the ground is all white,
The holiday season breeds joy and light,
Hot cocoa is made to warm up the night.

As the birds start to chirp, the bees start to swarm,
Flowers are blooming in all colors and forms,
Spring has arrived as the days start to warm.

Summer has come, hot days are here,
The beach is calling with good times and cheer,
Take a walk with a friend on an evening so clear.

A season of color - orange, yellow and red,
The best time of year or so it's been said,
All eyes on New England as the trees start to shed.

Red Winged Blackbird (46)

Red tips on the wings, he's easy to see,
A dark and shy guy, perched in the reeds,
Watching all passers-by, the hes and the shes.

Lake (56)

On a bright and clear day, you can see to its floor,
Reflecting so clearly, that which it sees, hears and more,
A collector of secrets, from all those gracing its shores.

60 Degrees (64)

In the middle of winter, snow on the ground,
It's the nicest of days, spring warmth is found,
Make the most of these hours, while they're around.

Fresh Air (65)

Step out the door, get greeted by a breeze,
Cool and refreshing, it rushes through the trees,
An invisible force, with the power to please.

Rain (66)

Tiny wet drops like tears from an eye,
Refreshing when cool, other times we sigh,
A band of colors brings cheer, across a blue sky.

Snowflake (99)

Crystalline in design, unique is each one,
Catching one on your tongue, is great child's fun,
Like manna, its flavor, can be any which one.

71

Snail's Pace (121)
So slow at times, it can be painful to view,
So slow it is, that racing proverb's not true,
It can take days to go from point one to point two.

Waterfall (134)
Gushing down to create, a white liquid wall,
A source of great power, there to serve all,
A gift of nature, from the short to the tall.

Sunny and Snowing (138)
Off little crystals airborne, shining so bright,
Reflecting the rays and spreading the light,
Takes off the chill, a heartwarming sight.

Seashells (140)
A rainbow of colors, shapes and size,
Some even have a hidden surprise,
The waves and tides bring them to our eyes.

Whale Watch (142)
Setting out from the cape, on a small boat,
Seeking out whales and items that float,
Our luck is unknown, and that's all she wrote.

Gust of Wind (147)
Blowing so hard, tree branches crack,
If venturing out, have a bud watch your back,
All loose objects are subject to attack.

Horizon (150)
Off in the distance, a lovely sunset the best,
Where some journeys end, way out in the west,
A worthwhile view on each day of my quest.

Azure Blue (175)
Look up at the sky, it's the clearest of days,
No haze in the air, warm are the sun's rays,
Friends stroll in pairs, with only smiles today.

Seashore (153)
Waves crash on the beach, gems in the foam,
There are colorful shells and driftwood to take
home,
A place to relax, to let yourself freely roam.

Hiding Place (57)
Tucked away somewhere, scarce and remote,
Lack of knowledge it's guard, like a wide and deep
moat,
Thousands exist, each one unique and of note.

Winter Wonderland (163)

Standing out on my deck, surveying fresh snow,
Six inches about, white frosting for show,
Brings back memories, when I made snowballs to
throw.

The Squirrel in the Tree (109)

In a nest of fall leaves, at a very high height,
A gray critter looks out, in acorns he delights,
Who when feeling tame, puts screen doors in his
sights.

Song (111)

A collection of notes, sometimes coupled with
words,
An audible message, pleasant to be heard,
Known to more than man, like the whales and the
birds.

Robin on the Wire (176)

The sun is out, the warmth is quite fair,
Up on a wire, a robin surveys with care,
That's the first sign, that spring's in the air.

Stained Glass (185)
Colorful shards pieced into a design,
An intricate scene on a window so fine,
Who knew that sand could be truly divine.

The Moon (188)
High overhead, illuminating the night,
Reflecting the sun, its features shine bright,
Showing the way, like a guard made of light.

Woodpecker (197)
Black and white, with some touches of red,
Feathers come to a point, on top of its head,
The clatter it makes is one insects do dread.

Crack of Dawn (199)
Throw open the shade, the sky's getting bright,
Today's a new day, may it be a delight,
Creation's a joy, from the very first light.

Ocean (207)
An expanse so vast, to the horizon and more,
Waves so pretty and blue, bring treasures ashore,
Serene is the peace, of the breeze through my door.

Oasis (167)

Found on an island, all covered with sand,
Shaded by palms, a cool breeze that is grand,
With fresh water to drink, that's it's best gift on
hand.

Chirping Away (209)

Spring's in the air, with songs all around,
A grand symphony of short, pleasant sounds,
For on every tree branch, there are birds to be
found.

Fine Mist (222)

When it's ninety degrees, it refreshes and cools,
In the winter it chills, those in it are fools,
A shower and swim for those enjoying the pool.

The Little Bunny (252)

Hopping along, as innocent as can be,
Though shy and skittish, it's got the garden
munchies,
Heathery brown, with ears distinctive to see.

Gold Finch (267)

Zips through the sky, a bright little fellow,
Bright as the sun, a vibrant yellow,
A pleasing sight, with a song quite mellow.

Melodic Spring (269)
Peonies are pink and Iris are blue,
Carnations are yellow, daffodils too,
A melody of color, how gorgeously true.

Rustling Leaves (277)
On a cool fall day, there's a slow gentle breeze,
The fall colors rustle, high up in the trees,
Then float through the air, with a graceful ease.

Heat Wave (278)
Triple figure degrees, three days in a row,
The sun beating down, all paces are slowed,
Relief gets sought out, to the shade we all go.

Shade (279)
Whether under a roof or a tree canopy,
When the temperature soars, it's where we all flee,
To sip a cool drink, where the air is breezy.

Deluge (282)
Comes down in sheets and buckets overfilled,
Hits rather hard, to be in is no thrill,
The flashes and claps, are bright and quite shrill.

Summer Glee (283)

Sunshine and a breeze, with friends strolling by,
Doused by the waves, the tide is quite high,
Though ice cream will melt, one's spirits will fly.

Who's "Hoo"? (290)

In the hours past dusk, there's much to hear and see,
A pair of wings asks, "Who?", from way up in a
tree,
And with big round eyes, it watches over wisely.

September 21st (294)

As the daylight wanes, the leaves start to turn,
As the temperature drops, the holidays get yearned,
As colors abound - with songs of joy, cold is
spurned.

Fireflies (272)

Little flickers in the dark, so yellow and bright,
Flying specks of gold, which make a path in the
night,
Though it's hot and humid, they're a joy to one's
sight.

Food

Coffee (16)
Dark and hot goodness from little brown beans,
A gush of steam is a sight to be seen,
Black or flavored, the choices are obscene.

Tea (20)
Spanning the globe and thousands of years,
With so many flavors, choosing's the fear,
Whether hot or iced, many hold this drink dear.

Chocolate (78)
A dark brown substance, often brought on a tray,
Can be enjoyed any time of the day,
The darker and purer, is perhaps the best way.

Sugar (89)
Little white crystals, so pleasant and sweet,
Sometimes it's in cubes, to suck on one is a treat,
If the world were that way, it would be quite a feat.

Barbeque (112)
For dinner tonight, cook outside we will,
Burgers and franks, roast some vegetables,
The only debate, is which side of the grill.

Vegetables (113)
Lettuce, onions, cauliflower and kale,
Potatoes, cabbage and carrots by the pail,
Turnips and parsnips, when roasted can't fail.

Fruits (114)
Apples and pears; grapes, peaches and dates,
Black, blue and straw - are berries so great,
Pineapples, mangos- that makes a tropical plate.

Pizza (126)
Countless toppings, meats and veggies so grand,
A few types of crust: deep, thin and pan,
The sauces are two, with several cheeses on hand.

Cheese (128)
Gouda and Cheddar, Havarti and Brie,
Romano and Blue, Parmesan and Colby,
The tasting of cheese is a global journey.

Grinder (149)
On artisan bread, stuffed to the gills,
Meats and veggies, cheese and dressing the fills,
So tall in fact, each bite exceeds a mouthful.

Dessert (165)
The meal's last course, it's sweet usually,
Candy and cake, or a plate of cookies,
Washed down by a drink, perhaps coffee or tea.

Garden (166)
Full of veggies, and fruits quite a few,
Gives produce all year, some is shared too,
With the rabbits and squirrels, come often they do.

Nuts (168)
Used in many ways, come with shells or in cans,
Walnuts and almonds, chestnuts and pecans,
Peanuts are a bean, remember that if you can.

Ice Cream (169)
Many flavors there are, new ones by the day,
While most make sense, some are to gross to say,
A flavor's net sales determines it's stay.

To the Last Bite (284)
The food was so good, it was beautifully cooked,
Perfectly seasoned, the salt was textbook,
Every bite was a hint, of a talented cook.

Cocoa (23)

A hot, dark drink to warm body and mind,
Topped with marshmallow, it's fluff white and fine,
On the coldest of days, liquid chocolate's divine.

Burned Toast (143)

Has lines that are black, charred is the way,
Some find this strange; it smells bad they say,
Homage to my grandfather, how he started each
day.

Sports & Games

Baseball (19)

A nine-inning battle, sometimes more,
From spring to fall and shore to shore,
A national pastime, it be one out of four.

Football (25)

Four quarters, sixty minutes of good rough fun,
Games always get played, in rain, snow or sun,
The super bowl is the game to crown number one.

Boxing (44)

A hand high and low, to block up and down cuts,
Toughest to absorb, is the blow to the gut,
A pop to the face, will keep any mouth shut.

Deck of Cards (122)

Base fifty-two and two jokers thrown in,
Games by the dozen, alone or with kin,
Hundreds of backs, in boxes or tins.

Ice Water in Veins (200)

With seconds to go, the game is all tied,
Make this shot here and it'll be bona fide,
With elation so great, please feel free to cry.

Ice Skating (204)
All across the ice with style and grace,
In sparkling garb, at a rather quick pace,
For national pride and a podium place.

Triple Crown (233)
At Churchill Downs, the journey begins,
The Preakness is next, the second leg to win,
History at the Belmont, get all your bets in.

At the Races (5.3.19 - 234)
It's a beautiful day to take in a race,
See all the big hats, with style and grace,
With just minutes to go, get all your bets placed.

Basketball (5.8.19 - 236)
Twenty-nine point five is the distance around,
Eight point five is the pressure in pounds,
An orb of glory as the seconds tick down.

Yankees (251)
Ruth and Gehrig, the big three and four,
DiMaggio, Mantle, kept centerfield well shored,
Rivera and Jeter, two of a modern-day core.

Here Comes the Pitch (266)
Thrown from the mound, to the plate it dashed,
Swung at with a bat, it's struck with a smash,
Then snared by a glove, when leather gets flashed

Cookie Jar Hands (183)
High on a shelf, full of round, dessert treats,
Chocolate, sugar, oatmeal raisin so sweet,
Scaling the walls is no easy feat.

Bat, Ball, Glove (263/264/265)
A long wooden stick, made of maple or ash,
Here comes the pitch, with the stick it's lashed,
If the hitter is lucky, he hits a long smash.

White leather covers, stitched with red string,
Held many ways, with speeds varying,
Mixing is the key to entice empty swings.

Made of leather - often black, brown or tan,
Used to catch the ball, by both players or fans,
A padded layer, extending one's hand.

Bullpen (116)
A group of strong arms, there to answer the call,
Left or right-handed, their job is to pick up the ball,
Bridging the gap, to some rising fastballs.

On the Bench (132)
Down the far end, where the coach hardly sees,
The second five sits, getting stiff knees,
Though when called on, the hardest workers they
be.

53 in the Bar (213)
The game draws to a close, the seconds tick down,
With a lead of ten points, the room lacks extra
sounds,
The bartender and I are the last two around.

USA

Corner Shop (14)

From bagels and donuts to coffee and tea,
A warm setting, with a new friend to see,
Each one is unique, in eats, air and glee.

USA (95)

A nation so broad, complex is its brew,
Of cultures, religions, landscapes and people too.
The mix is its beauty, coast to coast this is true.

Presidents Day (105)

They come, they go, four-year terms to the day,
No one can please all, it's a curse you might say,
Opinions aside, Happy Presidents Day!

Tax Day (110)

One day each year that everyone hates,
When money hard earned gets tossed to the state,
April 15th is this infamous date.

The Bounty Hunter (115)

On a sturdy old horse, gun at his side,
With a stash of posters, that he cleverly hides,
Though justice's the goal, in very few he confides.

New York (120)
A diverse entity, its boroughs are five,
With so many people, it's one mixed up beehive,
Where cultures do cross, and religions can thrive.

The Cowboy (124)
On horseback he's goes, often packing a gun,
The West is his home, with abodes more than one,
Herding cattle and horses, see the animals run.

New Orleans (129)
A city of culture: ethnic foods and jazz,
A crossroads of mixtures - creative pizazz,
Something for all, this city sure has.

Homage in Snow (145)
Named for a hill on the island Iwo,
Topped with a flag, much like years ago,
So awesome a sight, of packed ice and snow.

Philadelphia (151)
For brotherly love, this city is known,
In one hallowed hall, independence was grown,
Rung in by a bell, liberty was its tone.

Penny (155)

A small unit of change all over the West,
Bad ones turn up, like unwanted house guests,
A pretty one's nice, says one's luck is the best.

Steel Penny (156)

Of mostly copper, it's value one cent,
Though for one year, to bullets it went,
And steel was then used to mint every red cent.

Indian (157)

Those of red skin, with unique tribal names,
Images are widespread, profiles of fame.
A piece of our past, all removals bring shame.

Little Bookshop (158)

In a quaint little house, some have a cafe,
Walls lined with books, where readers come to play,
An author's eden, a place to go every day.

Fireplace (164)

It gives plenty of heat on a cold winter's night,
Lamps are left off, with the abundance of light,
Huddled with kin, is a neighborly sight.

Pilgrims (172)
Religious freedom is that which they seek,
In a land far away, many miles and weeks,
New friends and foes, high and low peaks.

Armistice (180)
The terms were drawn up in a hall in Versailles,
Delivered to a coach, clear cut with no guise,
Spawning parades, the sight of all eyes.

City Streets (181)
Bright paved routes with many dialects heard,
People all kinds, from the nice to the nerds,
Beware of each step and be a hawk to your words.

The Old Oak Tree (182)
A tree of legend, for many reasons,
A sign to plant corn for local Indians,
And for the charter one held, in a hollow within.

Stamps (190)
Squares of paper, with detailed designs,
Homages to the past, the artwork quite fine,
With deckled edges to create jazzier lines.

Gold Rush (194)
Down a mine shaft in the California dust,
Are seekers of fortune, for something of lust,
With two kinds of luck, success or go bust.

Pyramid (196)
A geometric shape rising out of the sand,
An unfinished one is on that bill in your hand,
Symbolism two-fold across cultures so grand.

The Write-In Line (198)
"For whom did you vote?", "I will not tell.",
All the candidates stink, that's more than just smell,
The write-in line is a gift, a blessing so swell.

The Right to Vote (218)
Endowed as sacred, a true cornerstone,
A secret process, anonymous and unknown,
Your choices are yours and should never be shown.

New England Weather (225)
Four distinct seasons, unique is each one,
With varying temps and its own brand of fun,
If you want it to change, just wait a bit, son.

Jury Duty (227/228/229)
A cast of characters, none of them thrilled,
With palpable boredom, the room overfills,
Silence abounds, testing patience and will.

A nine-hour day that makes sitting no fun,
Most of it is waiting, pass time everyone,
Could make those who are slow, jump up and run.

The process is dull, there's endless waiting,
Boredom flows well, when silence is king,
How is time passed, stare at the ceiling.

Memorial Day (237)
A day set aside, to reflect on the past,
To honor those fallen to build a country so vast,
By defending our rights, from the first to the last.

Bald Eagle (253)
Perched way up high, so it can see all around,
Scanning its land, from the clouds to the ground,
For miles and miles, there's much glee to be found.

Patchwork Quilt (254)
Of fabric pieces, all sizes of scraps,
Draped on a bed or around one it's wrapped,
Warms one to the core, when snow falls untapped.

New England (255)
Wait a few minutes and the weather will change,
Four distinct seasons, six states just as strange,
It's people and precepts make up a broad range.

River (259)
Winding through mountains, forests, farms and
hills,
For hundreds of miles, can make a trip a real thrill,
Interstate travel, before the roads became filled.

Sheriff (275)
Upheld the law, in times wild with sand,
On a horse or by foot, with a gun close at hand,
Alone or with men, a posse to command.

Stars and Stripes (58)
Red, white and blue; high up on a pole,
A sign of freedom, western values extolled,
A sight which brings warmth to our hearts and our
souls.

July 4th (98/271)
A day of great joy, games and sparklers,
Freedom is great, let's have a cookout for sure,
Our little gift, to aromatic fervor.

A day to celebrate the red, white and blue,
To bask in the freedoms, we hold dear and true,
With sparklers and games and a cookout or two.

Autumn in New England (159)
Six northeastern states, known for autumn leaves,
With four defined seasons, it's the fall color that's
cleaved,
The best in the world or so it's believed.

Lighthouse (189)
Through the fog, is a beacon so tall,
With a light and a horn, wards ships from a rock
wall,
On an isle its own, it's a savior to all.